CONTEMPORARY AUSTRALIAN MONOLOGUES

for Women

Edited by Emma Rose Smith
and Claire Grady

CURRENCY PRESS
SYDNEY

First published in 2017
by Currency Press Pty Ltd,
PO Box 2287, Strawberry Hills, NSW, 2012, Australia
enquiries@currency.com.au
www.currency.com.au

Reprinted 2020

Cataloguing-in-Publication data for this title is available from the National Library of Australia website: www.nla.gov.au.

Cover design Alissa Dinallo for Currency Press.
Internal design by Emma Vine for Currency Press.
Typeset by Emma Rose Smith for Currency Press.
Printed by Fineline Print + Copy Services, Revesby, NSW.

CONTENTS

FOREWORD

At Currency HQ, we love Australian plays and we welcome any opportunity to talk about them. Thankfully, so do our customers and we get a lot of calls from them asking for suggestions. One of the most common requests we receive is a recommendation for a monologue. We get so many, in fact, that we decided to collect our favourite contemporary monologues into a single package—and here it is.

The selection process has been great fun, though not without moments of heartbreak. Some difficult choices needed to be made and some favourites got dropped in our attempt to get the balance right. We've aimed for diversity in writing style, age of character and length. I hope we've got something here for everyone, whatever your age and whether you're preparing your monologue for drama school, a showreel, or an audition for a professional production.

In the following pages you'll find a refugee and a zookeeper. We've got Lindy Chamberlain-Creighton, on the night before she appeared in the witness box and Sappho, speaking to us 2700 years (roughly) after her death. There are grieving sisters and conflicted bridesmaids and activist haberdashers. The commonality is that they are all written by Australian playwrights. And they are all beautifully drawn characters.

The monologues are presented here in order of length. Dean Carey suggests in the Australian audition bible, *The Actor's Audition Manual*, that the ideal length for a monologue is between one-and-a-half to three minutes. The majority of monologues included here fall within that criteria. We have included some longer monologues—these are for students completing the individual performance for the end-of-school exams. Several of them can also be cut to suit your needs so I'd recommend that even if you are looking for a shorter monologue, take a look at the monologues towards the end of the book.

We have included a brief introduction to each piece to provide context to the monologues. These include the age of the character (wherever possible), along with notes about when and where the piece is set. These introductions, however, are intended as a starting point, and are not a substitute for reading the plays themselves. A paragraph cannot do justice to the nuances and subtleties of each of the characters that appear in these pages, who are further developed during the course of the plays in which they appear. We'd also recommend researching as much as possible on the world of the play to provide further context and depth to your performance. It's also important to note that we have slightly adapted some of the monologues, cutting other characters' lines, asides or directions that don't make sense without the context of the entire play. We have added a note to the monologue's introduction to show where this has happened.

When choosing your monologue, we recommend that you pick one that you feel an emotional connection to. This doesn't necessarily mean that you should only be choosing characters that share your own personal experience, but remember that to make the monologue work, you will need to find the emotional trigger. Be culturally sensitive. Choose wisely and trust your instincts.

And so, without further ado, here they are. We hope you enjoy the following monologues as much as we have enjoyed putting the book together.

Claire Grady, 2017

IRIS

From *The Hanging*

by Angela Betzien

Three 14-year-old girls from an exclusive boarding school go missing. One of them, Iris, turns up several days later, covered in scratches and with no apparent memory of what has transpired. In this passage, Iris is talking to Detective Flint, describing her friendship with the two others, Hannah and Ava. Ms Corrossi is their teacher. The Hanging *explores Australia's notion of lost children and throughout the play there is a sense of growing menace. There is an ambiguity around Iris—we never quite know when she is telling the truth.*

You don't know anything.

We've been friends forever. We spent the whole September break together. Hannah and Ava stayed at our property.

It used to be a farm before my father bought it for a song. There was a lake. It was millions of miles deep. When the farm went broke the farmer's daughter walked into the water. Just like Virginia Woolf. They never found her body, that's how deep it was. Diving down, the water changed from viscous green to inky black. It was so cold we'd get goosebumps on our breasts. And every day of the holidays we played The Farmer's Daughter. I always lost. I couldn't hold my breath. Hannah stayed under forever, for an eternity. I'd scream.

Hannah! Hannah! Come back!

Then she'd break through the surface like a beautiful swan.

Now it's all gone.

It's just a big, black, gaping mouth. [A coalmine.]

Ms Corrossi says we've swallowed the future.

She says we're beyond the tipping point.

We've already gone over the cliff but we've been running so fast that gravity hasn't caught up. We're suspended in mid-air. We haven't fallen yet, but we will. It's just a matter of time.

We're *doomed* and one day soon, *we'll pay for the sins of our fathers.*

TB

From *Prayer to an Iron God*

by Caroline Reid

Prayer to an Iron God *is a gutsy play set in a country town in Western Australia. TB's brother, Damien, has died by suicide and the play examines the impact of the suicide on those left behind. TB (or Tits and Balls) is a tough character in her early to mid 20s. Sniff is her boyfriend. The following is the opening monologue of the play and TB begins with her eyes shut.*

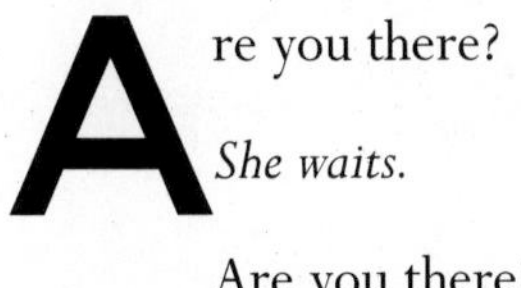

Are you there?

She waits.

Are you there?

She waits.

I wouldn't be scared if I opened my eyes and saw you.

Nothing but the wind is heard. She opens her eyes hoping, but not expecting, to see an apparition of her dead brother. She looks up, smiles.

I can see your face in the clouds. Eyes all wonky. Big open mouth. Looks like you're tryin to scare off planes. Tiny things they are from down here, flying in one ear and out the other. When the wind's up you don't hang around for long. Your face gets squished and it's just big fat cloud again. That wind's been up all week, turnin Mum inside out even more than usual. I told her about Sniff takin off. All she said was: 'Keep your chin up girl. He'll be back.'

I keep my chin up, I see you in the clouds. Always come back to you, little brother. Not a day goes by. Me and Mum arguin about whose fault it is the most.

Skunk reckons there's one good rain left before the heat really hits. [*She follows the slow movement of clouds with her head.*] There you go. Just big fat cloud again.

MARA

From *Jump for Jordan*
by Donna Abela

The matriarch of a Jordanian-Australian family, Mara never quite forgives her husband, the gentle and romantic Sahir, for bringing her to Australia. The 'little sticks in little jars' are the Australian native plants he grows for her. She is in her 20s and she is a recent migrant to Australia. Sahir has planned a home, on 'the highest block in the land' in Western Sydney, and a garden with native plants that will flower at Christmas. But the house isn't built yet and Mara is pregnant and unhappy.

Sahir, we had a house, my half of my father's house in Amman, in the capital city of a modern Kingdom. Now we have what? A cold and filthy bedsit on the other side of the world. You have work, you have friends at the factory, come home whistling nice happy tunes because you're thinking of that horrible block of wind and cow shit that you expect me to live in. What do I have? A landlady in yelling dresses who blocks the corridor with her bulk and sneers at my cooking. Strangers who get drunk on the steps and live in smelly dark rooms in sin. A husband who grows little sticks in little jars for a little garden that will never smell as sweet as the irises and jasmine you grew for me in Jordan.

Arabic! Speak Arabic to me!

Don't do this, Sahir, don't strand me in my own language, crying all day and unpacking nothing. I have nothing to put away in the home I don't have, the home not built yet for the baby on the way!

AISHA

From *Truck Stop*

by Lachlan Philpott

The following is the opening scene. Aisha is 14 and Kelly and Sam are her friends, who are sneaking out of school to solicit sex at the local truck stop. It is based on a true story. In Truck Stop, *Philpott is giving voice to those who often go unheard. The language is authentic but heightened—there is a gritty poetry to the dialogue that is evident in the monologue below.*

In the middle of the quad that day Kelly walks up to Sam and slaps her in the face. Slap like a cracking whip. Everyone hears it. Stops.

Sam shakes her head, turns away, turns back, runs at Kelly, pushes her to the ground, punches her in the face. Kelly snatches Sam's hair, twists it round her wrist, pulls her by the hair, looks her in the eye, spits in her face.

Kids circle them, phones held overhead.

Teacher pushes through the ring, rips Sam and Kelly apart.

Teacher yells, spits anger in their faces. Two sides he's saying. Two sides to every story.

Everyone says that.

Miss Rowse, the headmistress, stands in front of the whole school and raves on about protection. The school gates protect you from the outside, your parents and your friends protect you, look out for you. Her voice drops to almost a whisper as she says *but you still need to protect yourselves*.

The story about the Truck Stop has more than two sides.

Sam's side. Kelly's side. The truck drivers, their wives or girlfriends or mothers or sons.

Sam's mum, Kelly's mum, Sam's dad, the cop and the counsellor.

Me.

Now. Kelly doesn't speak to Sam. Kelly hardly speaks at all. You can split most things into halves. Movies, hours, oranges, cupcakes.

Friendships don't stand up so well.

MRS BUCKTIN

From *Jasper Jones*
adapted by Kate Mulvany
from the novel by Craig Silvey

It's 1965 and New Year's Eve in Corrigan, a small town in Western Australia. Teenage Laura Wishart has gone missing and Charlie Bucktin knows that she is dead. He is grappling to come to terms with the harsh realities of life in Corrigan. In this scene, Charlie has stumbled across his mother having an affair. In the stage direction, it says that Mrs Bucktin speaks numbly, though it is anger that seems to be her driving motivation up to this point.

Your father and I don't love each other anymore. We … lost it somewhere. He's more in love with that bloody book than he is with me.

You think he's sitting in that nursery mourning our dead child? No. That's my job. He's writing a book.

[It's] the Great Australian Novel, Charlie.

I reckon it's set in a town of never-ending fucking silence. Silence and space. Dead paddocks and dried-up dams and a bunch of ghosts covered in dust walking around a place where nothing ever changes. It just doesn't fucking change. Stinking men and bored women and incessant heat and filthy flies and fucking on a back seat. Just to feel something, just to feel anything, just to escape the silence. It's about a town that kills women. Murders little girls. A town that even my baby daughter didn't want to be born into. I reckon that's what it's about. Your father's Great Australian Novel. Maybe he's wrapping it all up with a happy ending? That'd be nice, hey? But you know what I reckon, Charlie? I reckon he hasn't written a damn word. Because that's his way. Silence and space.

I won't be here tomorrow. I'm leaving Corrigan.

I'm going.

Look after your dad for me.

And make sure he looks after you.

One day you'll understand. About all this.

You're a good man, Charlie. I love you, my darling. Sorry.

AUGUSTA

From *The Turquoise Elephant*
by Stephen Carleton

Set in Sydney in the near future, The Turquoise Elephant *is an Absurdist play and there should be nothing small about the performances. Augusta Macquarie is formidable matriarch and an environmental vandal. We're not sure of her age but it could be 'Ninety. A hundred. Immortal.' In this scene she is speaking to a crowd as the Interim Governor General. She walks into the limelight, arms outstretched to receive the glory in Eva Peron style. She exults in the moment.*

They say all the grand certainties are dead. God. History. Truth. All dead. The weather—the seasons as we know them. Apparently even capitalism itself is dying!

Laughter.

Please! You wish!

Applause.

Oh, yes, it's an apocalypse, people! Well, you don't hear them complaining about the end of days in the wheat fields of Greenland. The Chinese and Mexicans are cloud seeding. Saudi Arabia is pioneering drought-resistant crop technology. They're growing food in dust bowls! If this is the apocalypse, I say bring it on!

It's time to embrace change and make practical preparations for our future.

Those of us gathered in this room are the solvers of the world's problems.

We are the pioneers.

The ones whose business acumen and innovation will help humanity adapt to the change that Mother Nature is wreaking upon us, even as we speak.

Loud cheers.

The timing is urgent.

There are actually those—the enemy within—who would have us live in permanent terror and apprehension about the sort of change we are proposing this evening. Purveyors of doom who threaten us with violence for finding solutions to the world's problems!

Laughter and applause.

Well, we're not afraid of you!

Cheers.

To this homegrown enemy, to the faceless and so-called 'cultural' terrorists, this 'Front', these Turquoise militants, I say … up yours! We are the history-makers. We are the gatekeepers. We are the future and we are unstoppable!

JOMANA

From *Tales of a City by the Sea*

by Samah Sabawi

Jomana is a Palestinian journalist in her late 20s, born and raised in a refugee camp in Gaza. The play takes place in the 2008 / 2009 bombardment of Gaza. This scene takes place in Shifa Hospital, Gaza City. Jomana has learned that it was her neighbours, and not her parents, that were killed and injured in a recent blast. In the monologue below, Jomana addresses the audience directly.

I have a confession to make
I stand between shame and relief
I breathe …
The missiles missed this time
Truth is they didn't really miss
Someone's house is destroyed
But not the house I know so well
Someone's family is grieving
But not the one whose name I carry
I linger …
I linger between shame and relief
I breathe …
I … breathe …
I tell myself
This flesh, torn and scattered
Is not flesh I have ever embraced

I soothe myself
Nor are these small lifeless hands
The ones with a crayon I've traced
I … breathe …
This time …
The missiles missed those
Whose names are engraved on my lips
This time they didn't stop those hearts
Beating in my chest
They live …
And I breathe …
But I must confess
Every time the bombs fall
I want answers
Where did they strike?
Which street did they blow up?
Which neighbourhood did they destroy?
Which lives did they steal?
Aware of my guilt I whisper a prayer
Dear God,
Please don't let it be the ones I know
Dear God
Please don't let it be the ones I love
Dear God …
Ya allah …
Ya allah …
Ya allah …
And when it's over
And while a less fortunate family weeps
I stand between shame and relief
I breathe …
I breathe …
Thank God my loved ones were spared …
This time!

CELIA

From *The Peach Season*

by Debra Oswald

The Peach Season *has its basis in the myth of Demeter and Persephone. Celia is a peach farmer and mother to teenage Zoe. Her husband was killed in a car accident and Zoe is her only, adored daughter who she tries desperately to keep safe from harm. It seems inevitable that Zoe will run away and Celia ultimately realises that the greatest act of love is in giving Zoe her freedom. The following monologue is cut from two sections of the play. The first part is before Zoe has left, and the other after she has been found and Celia has learned to let her go.*

I'm all right in the daytime, y'know.

I know I'm an anxious person.

But two in the morning I wake up and—oh…

[The dangers] ooze up while I'm asleep until my brain is awash with panic.

The world is a dangerous place. Most people have the luxury of ignoring that.

When Zoe was born, they put her on my chest and she looked me straight in the eye. The challenge was there. I must protect this person.

I never wanted to infect her with the fears.

I watched her climb trees and dive off highboards.

Now there's so much… At night, terrifying thoughts—toxic residue—it silts up in here.

A quarter of all road fatalities are in the fifteen- to twenty-year-old age group. Many girls contract human papilloma virus during their first sexual experience. Youth suicide—increased thirty-five per cent over the last ten years. The average age of first heroin use has dropped from twenty to sixteen.

If I list them, meditate on them, they won't happen. I know that's crazy.

Night-worrying—it's the mother's voodoo. So in the daytime I can be normal and sturdy and get on with things.

I can see that Zoe is stronger. She doesn't let unimportant things get to her like she used to. But sometimes, when we talk on the phone, it only takes two syllables and I can hear if she's wretched. That blackness in her voice.

At night I still catalogue dangers, but now I add to the conjured scenes. I rewrite the stories—imagine Zoe escaping trouble by her good judgement, quick wits, strong heart.

I urge her to be strong. As if all my hours of worrying and urging will distil and harden into a small, bright amulet she can wear around her neck to protect her wherever she is.

IRINA

From *Parasites*

by Ninna Tersman

Irina is a 15-year-old asylum seeker. Parasites *is set in the common room of a refugee shelter in the present day, and it's midnight. Irina is wearing a white long nightgown and she is disorientated and feverish. She is speaking to her friend Behrouz but she is confused—she thinks he is her mother. She dreamt that she burnt her hands but in her fevered state, she believes it really happened. Throughout the scene, Behrouz tries to reason with her. We have cut his lines to create the following.*

I don't have a fever
No, it's just hot in here
It's summer, isn't it?
Where is Isaac?
His hands are so smooth
His palms are so pink
Are my palms like Isaac's?
As smooth
Why did he burn them?
My fingertips are all shiny
See
No patterns
All gone
I put my hands on the hot stove

Last night
It really hurt
The skin sort of—melted
Just like Isaac told me
And then he gave me some ice
Afterwards, to cool them down
It's great, now they have to start all over
I'm blank
They don't know who I am
I'm not in any database
Not here or anywhere
I'm like a baby
Newborn
Isaac told me how
His hands are soft and pink, like a baby's
It's because he already tried
In Europe
He's already tried to stay
He's in the database
And they didn't believe him there
They sent him back
On a chartered plane
Did you know that?!
Two guards held him and a third sprayed something in his face
When he struggled
They broke one of his fingers
He sat between them on the plane
In handcuffs
Did you know that?!
I've seen his scars
From the prison in his home country

Have you seen them?
On his back
They look like roads, or tracks—on a map
All over his back
He escaped from the military
He never showed it to the immigration officers in the country where he tried
Which country was that?
A very rich country
With too many people in it
He didn't think about it
He forgot to show them his scars!
Why didn't he show them?!
And now it's too late
Because he's in the system
Do you think they'll send him back from here too?
I need to water my tree
Nobody cares about the tree, but me!
It almost died!

THE DROVER'S WIFE

From *The Drover's Wife*

by Leah Purcell

The Drover's Wife *is a retelling of the classic Henry Lawson short story. Set in 1893, it takes place on an outback station. The drover's wife is heavily pregnant, with just her son and dog, Alligator, for company, when Yadaka arrives, a young Indigenous man on the run from the law. The two form a friendship. Here she is telling the story of the bullock, at the urging of her son Danny, to Yadaka. It's a great yarn but it also establishes her character: fierce and brave and funny. It also marks a turning point in her relationship with Yadaka and the growing intimacy between them. This monologue is intended for an Australian Indigenous performer.*

It was afternoon, just over a week and a bit now. I came outside to call Alligator.

I hadn't even got my nose out the front door when … Lord Almighty … I came face to face with this big bloody wild, grey bullock.

I froze, as it had. Both of us not sure what the other was gonna do, should do, could do.

Lucky for me, you kids were inside or out back and normally would have no reason to come around the front to enter the house.

A quick scan of the yard, no Alligator, good.

The bullock would have ripped him apart; horns the width of a grown man's arm span. Dog may be old but he's loyal, eh, a good protector.

So, I still haven't moved from the partial open door, still holdin' eye contact with the beast, its breath short and sharp.

You sat on the dirt floor drawin' in the loose sod from the day's foot traffic of adult, child and dog.

'Danny?' I whispered.

'Danny.'

Darn kid's so focussed on his penmanship.

'Daniel!' Finally.

'The gun. Now. Slow.'

Ya looked up in protest—

Ya rose slowly, grabbed the Martini Henry, which ya're taller than now, ya skinny malinky longlegs! And hands it to me—

I always have it loaded.

I slowly bring the gun up usin' the doorframe as my guide.

The laughter of me children was movin' now, to my right.

The bullock looks over, sees them and stomps. I step forth from the door, bringing its attention back to me. Takin' aim now right between the eyes of the beast … someone was gonna die!

Second stomp, so glad its animal instinct was to show its authority.

One eye closed, the other locked on my target … breath steady. The beast snorts: short and sharp … my children now silent and still … and time stopped …

One single shot …

Small trickle of blood between its eyes and the bullock drops …

[Dead.]

MAVIS

From *Mavis goes to Timor*

by Katherine Thomson, Angela Chaplin and Kavisha Mazzella

Mavis Goes to Timor *is the true story of an 86-year-old haberdasher from Yarrawonga who decided to pack up her sewing machine and move to East Timor in a bid to help East Timorese women. The following extract is taken from early in the play—but we have already learnt that Mavis is not a woman to sit by idly and silently when she sees injustice. The preceding stage direction reads: 'Images of a birthday party. Small hands being held by older ones, presents being handed over. Little children passing around food. Precious, simple moments. Everyone should be entitled to such fortune… Mavis is poised to cut the cake.'*

Well, thank you, children, and grandchildren, and great grandchildren, for giving me this lovely party. A really lovely party. I really don't know why you're making such a fuss, it's not that hard to get to eighty-six, all you have to do is keep breathing. Thank you all for your gifts and all the delicious food, we mustn't let any of it go to waste. Now I do have something to say to you all. Something I've been waiting to say until I got you all together. You've all been wondering why the film crew's here, and that's because… well… I've decided to go to East Timor.

Silence.

[*Waving the knife*] Well. I might just cut the air.

Silence.

I've still got to work out the nuts and bolts, but look. [*Pulling out a hand-made book*] Someone's made me a home-made dictionary, everything I'll need to know in the language they speak there, Tetum. So I'll be right. I'd like to give the women up there something to do. Something to do other than grieve.

Silence.

I can teach them to sew and cut out patterns. I know what you're thinking—I've never used a pattern for any of you lot in my life, but that's just me. So the idea being the women can get involved, and make some income, and become self-sufficient. Steve and his crew are going to make a little documentary about it. About my trip. About East Timor.

Pause.

Which is, as I said… where I'll be going. Quite soon actually. So you won't have a lot of time to get used to it.

Pause.

You've only got to go out on that footpath right now and look at what we all throw out—three-quarters of that stuff the East Timorese could use. And what with the GST coming in… my shop's going to be… All the bits and pieces I sell, I'm likely to drown in paperwork.

JOJO

From *Beached*

by Melissa Bubnic

Jojo, in her mid-40s, is the doting mother of 18-year-old, 400 kilogram, reality TV subject Arty. She is being interviewed for the reality TV show in the following monologue, which appears towards the end of the play, just before Arty goes in for his gastric bypass surgery.

His dad? [*She snorts.*] Do you think the snort works? I don't wanna look bogan.

Maybe it should be more of... y'know, like a lion roar so I'm more powerful woman instead of... I know! I'll do a... y'know, a—

She sweeps her hand in a dismissive gesture.

A sorta 'piff!'. A 'sweep and piff!' and that'll look more like it's of so little consequence to me I just 'sweep and piff!'.

Beat.

She composes herself.

His dad? [*She sweeps and piffs.*] I knew all along he was no prize. Five feet nothing and eyes pointing any which way but straight. But I knew I was no prize either and it didn't matter 'cause he chose me. And you get a lifetime of never being chosen and when it happens, it makes a fool of you. You start believing in fairytales of happy ever after and maybe you're the swan after all because you're a fool, right? He left when Arty was three, none of this 'I'm going out for ice-cream or smokes or anything', he just… gone. At first I thought maybe he'd been murdered and it was the police who had to tell me I'd been dumped. I didn't cry but I shut down a bit. For a long time. Couldn't understand what I'd done wrong. I mean, I know how I am… but I tried to be different. Quiet. No trouble. Dinner ready. House clean. Beer in the fridge. And I'd replay over and over every single thing I did wrong—the couch cover too floral, shoulda seen a podiatrist about my feet, if I'd made him steak more—but y'know what really twists the knife in your gut? It's that you shoulda known better. You shoulda known he'd leave 'cause life isn't some TV show were people love you for who you are and buy you flowers on your anniversary. I don't have Hollywood skin and shiny hair and legs from here to eternity. I'm Joanne Arthur and this is the real world and I'm not complaining. I'm luckier than most 'cause I've got my boy, don't I?

She is crying.

I'm just so lucky. Really I'm just… I'm very, very lucky.

LUCY

From *Secret Bridesmaids' Business*
by Elizabeth Coleman

It's the night before Meg and James' wedding and 34-year-old Lucy, one of Meg's bridesmaids, has heard a rumour that James is having an affair. With the other bridesmaid. Lucy is addressing the audience directly here, and has just been convinced by the maid of honour, Angela, to wait for confirmation before voicing her suspicions. She prides herself on being a straight shooter and is torn between the risk of ruining her friend's wedding day because of an unfounded rumour and her fear that her friend will ruin her life if she doesn't tell her the truth.

Go on, look at me like that if you want, but I'm just trying to be a good friend here. It's not like I'm enjoying this… I can think of a lot more fun ways to spend a day, believe me—but real friends tell the truth. End of story. And it's all very well to hide behind niceness and lame excuses, but—Oh look, maybe that's not fair. Stuff it, I don't care—Angela's another one who's got this whole wedding thing way out of whack…

Frustration tempered by amusement

If you ask me—and I know you didn't—weddings are toxic. And I'll tell you why. Because they force decent people to lie. I mean, who can honestly say to another person, 'Yes, I know for certain that I'll forsake all others for the rest of my life?'

She gives a little laugh: What a ridiculous notion.

No-one, that's who. If you ask me, the vows should go, 'Right now I feel like forsaking all others, but let's consult again further down the track…'

Amused for a moment, then she remembers the situation, and her anger returns.

Jesus, if I saw James right now… Why ask Meg to marry him if he can't even keep his dick in his pants while they're engaged…?

She meets the audience's collective eyes.

Oh, yeah yeah, I know what you're thinking. Some couples can be happy forever. Well, they've won life's lottery. Half their luck. But the rest of us have to keep buying tickets…

And buying, and buying, and buying… Sometimes I feel like I'm running out of raffle books… Jesus, men have done terrible things to me, but I've treated them badly too. I've been unfaithful to a boyfriend once…

Thinking .

No, technically twice, and I'm not proud of that. But you know what else? I have *never* been unfaithful to a *friend*. Because friendship's too important to stuff around with. So, alright—I can wait till Kate rings, and I can cross all my fingers and toes that it isn't the same James, but if it *is*… I've never kept a friend in the dark—and wedding or no wedding, I'm not about to start.

PHOEBE

From *Sunset Strip*

by Suzie Miller

In this scene, 36-year-old Phoebe is speaking to her sister Caroline, who has recently returned to her childhood home after treatment for breast cancer. It is the day before her wedding and her young children, who have been taken away from her due to her drug dependence, are coming home. Caroline has just discovered that Phoebe is marrying Teddy, a man Caroline fell pregnant to while a teenager, resulting in an abortion. Caroline is protective of her sister (and of herself). She is struggling to be supportive of her sister but is sceptical about Teddy's character. Phoebe senses Caroline's reservations.

You might think you know Teddy
But you don't

You have no idea
He is a kind, gentle man
I know he's flawed
But I don't believe in perfection
I hate perfection
The chinks in him are lovely to me
His scar tissue made him who he is
So he can't cope sometimes
He's passionate

And unpredictable
But—
And you listen to me carefully Caroline
He is completely mine

I don't expect you to ever understand this
Know how I could choose him
A warm, pained, flawed, difficult man
But I know him
His softness, his nightmares, his self-hatred
I understand that Caro

Teddy and I have travelled to hell and back
And it is nothing noble
Nothing you can blame on chance
On lack of luck
It's purely the fuck-up of who we are

My children are coming home today after being in a stranger's home
Because their mother was deemed not good enough
A marred mother
Junkie mother
Sneered at by Social Services
A maternal failure
The only real job I've had

But I'm the only one who knows them
Really knows them
I know what song to sing when Lila's scared
Understand when Finn gets anxious
That he needs a big tickle and a hug
I'm their mum
And that counts for something

I don't care what everyone says
Because those two little people
They're perfect
The two things I got right
So I don't need all the judgement
Because together we make
A good little family
The three of us and Teddy

I can't lose them Caro
I will fight to my death to get them back

And Teddy understands
He's seen me with them
Seen me as a mother
Fiercely loving them
Understands I need all of us to be a family
He knows how afraid I am
And he isn't running from my fear
He sees it
And understands it
Because he has it too

He might not be a big city man
And yes he has a past littered with disaster
But all that is nothing
Compared to how I feel about him
How we touch each other

And I don't care about the past
A past that has you in it
I don't care—

He told me everything
Yep
We have no secrets
My only relationship
With no secrets

MEDEA

From *Black Medea*

by Wesley Enoch

Enoch's adaption of Euripides' Medea *blends Ancient Greek culture and Indigenous storytelling. In Enoch's play, Medea was raised in an Indigenous settlement but turned her back on her culture when she married Jason, a 'blackfella in a suit' from the city. Their marriage wasn't happy—he was violent and eventually threw her out. As in the original, her revenge is to kill their child. We have cut some text from the original to create this monologue. This monologue is intended for an Australian Indigenous performer.*

Give me a hair and a fingernail and I will curse you, Jason. Something with your sweat and I will curse you. Everything you have done to me, come back to haunt you ten times bigger. I want you to feel empty. The kind of emptiness I feel without you. I want you to wake up every morning and feel a part of you is missing. I want you to search and everywhere you look to see me… whenever you close your eyes to see me. Let the spirits hear me curse… let everything you love hurt you. Wherever love is inside you let it cause you pain, from the sharp hard jabs to weeping bedsores.

Let every time you love be like a knife between your ribs. Let no type of love be safe from my curse, not the love of a woman nor the love of a son.

I want you alive, I want you to feel an emptiness for as long as you live. I want you to carry the torment to your deathbed, alone and unloved. I want you to regret your life and when you die I will separate your bones and speak your name, and force your spirit to wander aimless without a home.

My revenge is born, already born, for I have given birth.

Spirits, this is my son. I have failed him. He has never known his Land, never left a footprint. I have abandoned him to follow his father. I have kept from him his songs and dances. I have denied him his family. Though he has tasted the spirit from my breast I have refused him his place in the Land. I've gone mad with living in two worlds.

In this long dark night I see it clearly—if he stays, he will become a copy of his father. He will grow up bruising the ones he loves, his children will live in fear, he will be another wandering soul. A mother's love will not allow it.

Spirits, the moon pulls me like the tide, I will not allow the sun to rise for him another day in this house. Before this night is through, my son will be freed, before the next day dawns, my son will know the spirits of his Land. I will take him.

Tonight I'm coming home. Let no man stand in my way.

SAM

From *SHIT*

by Patricia Cornelius

The character note at the beginning of the playscript reads: 'There's not a single moment when the three young women transcend their ugliness. They don't believe in anything. They're mean, downmouthed, downtrodden, hard bit, utterly damaged women. They're neither salt of the earth nor sexy. They love no-one and no-one loves them. They believe the world is shit, that their lives are shit, that they are shit.' In this scene Sam is speaking to the other two characters, Billy and Bobby. They have been through the same (or similar) shit—there should be an implied complicity and no fear of judgement. We have cut some of their lines, and Sam's, to create this monologue.

I'm with this family. They've got kids, two girls older than me, and a boy. About the same age as me. I'm four, I think, maybe more. I haven't been with them long. They're nice to me. I'm not hungry. We're at the beach and I've never been at the beach before and I don't like it much. The sand hurts between my toes and the water stings because my legs have got sores on them. I'm watching the boy, the pretty boy. They tell me he's my brother and them girls are my sisters but they're not.

He's full of himself, so full, full to overflowing with himself. They love him. They love him this family. His sisters do anything he wants and he wants a lot. He orders them about. He stands with his hands on his hips and shouts. Sometimes he smacks them and leaves a red mark on their skin and then he cries because he's sorry he's hurt them. They kiss him and kiss him and his head falls back and he giggles, the pretty boy, beautiful really, laughs and laughs. His father picks him up. He's told me he's my father too.

He picks up the boy and swings him up on his shoulders and he stands at the water's edge. He points out to sea, the father does, as if he's saying to the boy, this is all yours for as far as you can see. The mother joins them, smiling up at them, her eyes for the boy, the boy, the boy is everything. Now his sisters are dancing around, adoring him. There's this terrible noise and it pierces their ears and it disturbs the peace this terrible noise and I can't believe it, it's come from me. A scream has come up like spew from deep inside of me. They look and when they see that the noise is mine, they laugh, and are drawn back to the beautiful boy, forgetting me. Later the boy is alone playing a game in the shallows. He's giving orders to the waves as if they're his men and he's leading them to shore. He's lost completely in his imagining, nothing to worry him, to distract him, to disturb him from this world he's in, a world I've never been in, never, not once, not even for a second. Suddenly a wave larger than the rest comes and topples him, and here's my chance.

She puts her hand out as if to hold down the boy's head.

I got him.

Didn't stay with that family long. They didn't like me.

She laughs.

LINDY CHAMBERLAIN-CREIGHTON

From *Letters to Lindy*

by Alana Valentine

The following is a verbatim piece, based on an interview playwright Alana Valentine conducted with Lindy Chamberlain-Creighton. Lindy, a Seventh-day Adventist, was falsely accused of murdering her child in 1980 and underwent a trial, not just by the Australian judiciary system but also the media and the Australian public. The public pronounced her guilty before she got to the witness box. She is accustomed to being called a liar.

The night before I went into the witness box. As soon as I went into this room, this room where we were staying in Darwin, I thought, 'There's something in here'. We were in Darwin, it was roasting, there was air-conditioning in this room but it didn't go very low. But in this room I went into … it was like walking into a room with the freezer turned on. And the minute I walked in all the hairs on the back of my neck stood up. When I turned the light on there was nothing there. Michael had gone out to the other room. And so I turned the light out again, and that's when something heavy pushed on my chest to choke me. And I thought immediately, 'This is what my dad has described when he'd worked with people who thought they had evil in their house'. All I could think of was that he or somebody had said, 'If you repeat God's name then it will go'. But to begin with I could not even formulate the word in my head. I had to really fight until I could say it in my mind and then out loud and then I could move again and then I could say it louder and louder and I grabbed my Bible which was beside me and held onto it. From then on I slept with my Bible under my pillow. Sometimes I'd go into that room and I'd start to feel it and then I'd grab the Bible and it would go. And as I said Jesus' name over and over again the temperature of the room started to rise, the weight came off me and I could breathe again.

If you can't or won't or you don't want to believe me that's your prerogative. But you don't have to believe in physical evil the way I do to try to understand the evil that was being done in the world around me. There is evil that is supernatural and there is evil that is injustice. Well, that injustice tried to choke me to death. It was newsprint. It was the words you whispered or gossiped or the jokes you made. All of that balled up and became injustice. This grotesque series of lies and spite and rumour and human evil tried to smother my sense of belief in good and had me by the throat. Don't deny that it happened to me. Whatever name you give it, if it ever has you by the throat, let's talk again afterwards.

EMMA THE GREEK

From *At Sea, Staring Up*

by Finegan Kruckemeyer

Emma the Greek is the Icelandic character in Finegan Kruckemeyer's magical realist play about love and loss. In the following monologue, she is addressing the audience. She is 19 and her brother later tells her that she is 'terrible magic and carries death with her'. She left school when she was 14 to fish with her papa. In this scene, her father and brothers have some small lines of dialogue which we have here changed into reported speech, delivered by Emma in italics. If the following extract isn't long enough for your needs, Emma has a number of other monologues in the play that could lengthen the piece.

In the two weeks that me and my father and my two brothers are lost at sea, we floated a great distance. At one time on the tenth day, a large wave smashed a hole in the side and we had to take turns sitting on that bench and blocking it with our backs, and with our bottoms. I felt scared whenever it was my turn—my bottom was like bait I thought, for something in the sea. I did not wish my bottom to be eaten.

They call me Emma the Greek, but I am not Greek. I am olive-skinned though, and in Iceland this is odd enough for a nickname.

I cannot ask my mama the truth, because the sea carries no messages to the ones who lie at the bottom of it. Or even if the sea does do this, it does not bring back to the surface the replies.

In the two weeks, we shared a little food that we saved from the trawler before it went down. We throw tin cans into the lifeboat quickly and my brother said: *Not those ones Emma the Greek.*

And Papa said: *Don't talk bullshit, Paddy. Food is food. Hurry up or I leave you here.*

Papa is unforgiving and a taskmaster, we say. But he saved us all from my mama's ocean and it is for this I have no problem with him. Thank you Papa.

On the twelfth day, my oldest brother Ulli said: *One of us will not survive.*

And this was the biggest surprise, as Ulli has not said a one word for nine years. The doctor said he had a black hole grow in his brain one day, like exist in outer space, and the black hole sucked up all the words he had ever learnt in the twenty-two years before this, and then he has no more words. But I thought another thing—I thought was Ulli waiting for the right words.

On the last day, Papa says this is the coldest night coming and snow sat on the water around us, and we did not have to fear about the hole in the boat because the ice formed across it and blocked it—amazing. But Papa says: *This is the coldest night, boys and girl. And Emma the Greek does not stop shivering.*

I am okay Papa.

But they all take their jackets off and lay them on me, and I am too tired to argue, and I feel for the first time in days, warm. 'Why do they not make a normal jacket that is three jackets thick', I think. 'This is a great invention.'

And then I go to sleep, and as my eyes are closing, I see Papa and Paddy and Ulli in their t-shirts, and they are sitting together at the end of the boat, huddled together, and Papa is rubbing both their shoulders like a great big bear. He is a very good father.

And later I wake up when we hit the land, and I smile at Papa and Ulli and Paddy. And two of them look at me. But Paddy has blue skin and a look that is not for us anymore, but for Mama now. He can talk to Mama now, I understand this straight away. And so before we tie the boat and step ashore, we give him to the sea.

Goodbye, Paddy Blue Skin.

EVE

From *Myth, Propaganda and Disaster in Nazi Germany and Contemporary America* by Stephen Sewell

First performed in 2003, this play is a political thriller written in reaction in 9/11. Eve is American and sophisticated, beautiful and talented. She is a successful television writer. She is married to Talbot and she wants to have a baby. In this scene she is speaking to her therapist. If you need a longer monologue, Eve goes on in this scene to speak about America as a dangerous child and there are also several other excellent monologues in the play.

I want to be saved; I want my life to be saved, to be given some meaning, and I know another person can't do that for you, but I can't do it for myself. I can't, I've tried, but I can't.

I suppose I am angry, but it's so far down, I'm barely aware of it. I hate this, this floundering. I read this thing the other day, about self awareness—did you read it? That they're trying to write software for machines to have self awareness—isn't that a strange idea?—and the reason is to try to improve their mobility, because if a machine isn't really aware where it is in an environment, then it can't really navigate properly—So the idea is to write a program which allows the machine to locate itself in an environment—and that's a kind of self awareness; and so there I was thinking, is that all it is? All this goo in the middle of us, all this—who am I, where am I going, what does it mean?—all that stuff that's kept the motor of our civilization going for the last three thousand years—is just so I can get from the front door to the supermarket and back—And then I got a flash of one of those endless repetitive things—one of those Escher moments as I saw myself seeing myself seeing myself, all of us caught in a kind of transparent sphere of consciousness expanding at the speed of light—And you just wonder, don't you?—is Douglas Adams right, and the answer is 42? Well, he'd know now, wouldn't he; or he wouldn't, he wouldn't if he's just gone to dust, gone to cosmic dust disappearing into the darkness, and if machines can locate themselves in an environment, will they start wondering what it all means, too? And when they break down and decay, will they rage against fate and feel betrayed and alone? Will they feel angry that something has given them the ability to locate themselves in an environment, but never told them why they're there?—Am I making sense? Is any of this making sense?

No. No, it doesn't make sense; and if tomorrow a little green man from outer space arrived in New York and addressed the United Nations and said, 'I'm here to tell you the reason why you're here, and the reason why you're here is that five billion years ago a superior intelligence planted you as part of a strategy to fight the eternal war against the despicable Trogs', that wouldn't make any sense either, because that's not the kind of sense we want.

To know who we are, to not feel so alone.

EVE

From *Minefields and Miniskirts*
by Terence O'Connell
based on the book by Siobhán McHugh

Minefields and Miniskirts *is a verbatim piece based on true stories of the women who played a part in the Vietnam War. Eve is a volunteer. The following monologue is taken from two scenes of the play, and follows Eve from her decision to sign up to her arrival in Vietnam. She is telling the story retrospectively, from her home just around the corner from the Vietnamese strip in Richmond, Melbourne.*

It was a Saturday. We lived in the big house next to the Church of England in a leafy suburb. My father was the Minister. My mother ran the Ladies' Church Auxiliary and I learnt about serving others from them. I'd had my time of rebellion, of fluffy ducks and discoteques, marijuana and midnight swims, but I'd returned to the fold. Even though I was still searching for some sort of freedom, some mad idea of a 'Girls' Own' adventure. Here I was, in the kitchen with my mother, helping ice the cake for my wedding to a really nice boy from the Church Fellowship. On the wireless was an interview with someone from the World Council of Churches, talking about how they were looking for volunteers to go to Vietnam. I said, 'I'm so sorry, Mum, but I can't get married now'. I was already imagining myself with my Pan Am cabin bag, winging my way to Saigon…

I came out of the airport, got into a cyclo and was whirled into that incredible traffic.

A surging sea of motorbikes, bicycles and broken-down cars where there appeared to be no road rules at all. The noise was deafening, the filth, the smell, people peeing in the street! I thought I saw bloodstains everywhere, but it turned out it was the juice of the betel nut that they'd spit out on the footpaths. Then I was in my miserable little hotel room, having a bit of a cry, wondering what I'd got myself into. I was sitting on the toilet and next to me was another toilet, a funny shape. I fiddled around with the knobs and suddenly this fountain sprung up. I thought maybe it was a baby bath so put my aching feet into it. I'd never seen a bidet before! A week later I was washing my smalls in it. But I pulled myself together, said a prayer, put on a brave face and walked out into my new world. Alleyways with stall after stall of fabulously-coloured Thai silks, markets with vats of twitching eels, buckets of live frogs, piles of pigs' ears and snouts. Beautiful, young bar girls and drunken soldiers spilling out of nightclubs. I walked past Uncle Sam's Bar 'n' Grill. I turned a corner into Tu Do, and there were little children, all with their hands blown off, begging. Saigon was a street of walking wounded and I thought then, I'll do my best for these poor children if it's the last thing I ever do.

PIP

From *Things I Know To Be True* by Andrew Bovell

At 34, Pip Price is the eldest of the four Price children. The play takes place in the working-class suburban home of the Price parents. The following scene is set in the early morning and Pip is sitting in the garden, after jogging over from her own home nearby. The garden is complete with a Hills Hoist, a lemon tree, a lawn, roses, a shed up the back and an ancient eucalypt. No-one knows that she is there yet, but when her mother joins her Pip is going to tell her that she is leaving her husband. A brief moment of peace and introspection.

This garden is the world. Everything that matters happened here.

I kissed my first boy in that shed. I was nine. He was my cousin, Tom. Down from Port Augusta. I don't know if it counts if it was your cousin. But it was a kiss, nonetheless. He kissed me and then he put his hand down my pants. I don't know what he expected but I think he got a shock because he pulled it straight back out again. But I liked it. I got so excited that I bit his face. He started to cry and ran to his mother and I was sent to my room. And I don't know if it was because I bit him or because I liked having his hand down my pants. Somehow, I think Mum knew. I think she knew exactly why a girl bites a boy in the face. But then she always knew the things you didn't want her to know.

She caught us, me and Penny McCrea and Stella Bouzakis, with a bottle of sweet wine. We were in Year Nine and we snuck off from school at lunchtime. Penny had stolen it from her parents' drinks cabinet. We came back here and made a party of it, smoking those long coloured cocktail cigarettes as well. Thinking we were totally it. And suddenly Mum's standing at the back door. She was meant to be at work. She never came home for lunch. Never. But that day, when we're wagging school and drinking sweet wine in the backyard, she decides to come home. Stella got such a scare she started to vomit. Mum stuck her face in the compost pit and said, 'Vomit there, you silly girl'. I was grounded for the rest of Year Nine and never drank sweet wine again.

This garden is the world.

Family cricket and totem tennis tournaments. Hey Presto and cartwheels across the lawn. Fashion parades and sleepovers. Sunday barbecues. Eighteenth birthday parties. Twenty-firsts. Engagements. And even a wedding. Mine. It all happened here and more.

Once I saw her, Mum, bawling her eyes out and banging her head against the trunk of that tree. I was twelve. I had never seen her cry. Not once. Not even when her own mother died. And everything I thought was certain about the world changed. I went back inside and turned the television on. I was scared. What makes a woman cry like that? A mother. My mother. I didn't understand and I didn't have the courage to ask her. Now that I am a woman, married with children of my own, I don't need to, I know exactly why a woman bashes her head against the trunk of a tree.

This garden was the world.

ALISON

From *They Saw a Thylacine*
by Justine Campbell and Sarah Hamilton

They Saw a Thylacine *is set in Tasmania in 1936. Alison, 31, learnt to be a zookeeper from her father. On his death she applied for his role but instead the role was given to a returned soldier who neglects the animals, particularly Ben, the female thylacine. Ben has been locked out of her shelter repeatedly and has been crying at night. Alison can hear her from her cottage and on the night this scene is set, she decides to take action.*

I make a snap decision
I've got to break into the zoo
And somehow get her out
Of this ghastly night air
If I had Dad's spare set of keys
It would all be okay
But I don't I say
Out loud as I push my way through
The back door
A blast of wind
Hits me right in the face
As I shrug off my slippers
And in their place
Pull on my gumboots

Striding out into the dark
Through the howling of the wind
I hear her howling
Through her cage
And the rage I feel
Spurs me on through the back garden
And I begin to run
Pushing into the rain
Heading to the outer wall of the zoo
When above I hear a snap
From out of nowhere there's a thud
Back of my neck
And I fall to the ground sliding into the mud
For a moment I'm stunned
Dazed with the pain
My face is pressed into the dirt
I raise my arm to feel the back of my head
My hair is drenched from the force of the rain
And the force of the branch
Where it fell has left a split in my scone
I can feel a sharp stinging
From the cracking thud
As the split and the hair
Congeal with the blood with the blood with the blood
It's not too deep
I can tell
As I pick myself up
Survey the branch where it fell
It's large it's large—not too large not too large
I know I'll be fine
But this time I tread more carefully

On the path leading to the wall
I'm already drenched
And that momentary rush of adrenalin
I felt when I woke
Is waning
The pain in my head
Is strong is strong
Won't be long before I choke
Damn that lazy heartless bloke
I hear Ben call out
She'll be drenched
Chilled to the bone
I head past the big oak
Round the corner of the track
I can see the outline of the wall
And I hear her call
She's just on the other side
Locked in her front cage
I reach the caretaker's gate
And give it a shake
Though I know there's no use
A string of abuse escapes my mouth
You wanna know what I said?
It rhymes with 'brass hole'
Yes that's what I yelled and more
See the wall's a good seven foot high
It's gotta be
It's a zoo
We know why
It's to keep the crazies out
Well this crazy's going in

So I pull off my boots
Hoist up my nightie
And I stick my foot through the little gap
In the wrought-iron gate
The steel is slippery
Cuts into my socks
As I get towards the top
The wrought iron
Rocks off one of its hinges
The gate lunges backwards
My foot slips free
And I'm grasping it
With all my might
But I feel the other hinge
Beginning to go
And I know that if I don't let go
The gate's gonna break and so might my neck
So I bend my left knee
And swing myself free
And I squat on the outside of the wall as the rain pelts me hard
Down my head my neck my spine
Through the roar of the wind
I hear Ben whine
Just hang on, Ben,
Just make it through till dawn
And tomorrow I'll come straight to you
But all I can do is turn around and make my way
Back through the wind and the snow
My heart feels tight like it's being squeezed
I miss you, Dad
The goddamn goddamn goddamn keys

SONALI

From *Melbourne Talam*

by Rashma N. Kalsie

Sonali is a glamorous 29-year-old Indian woman living in Melbourne. The swing of her hips can be seen a mile away. The following is set in Sonali's messy room. She limps in, throws her bag down, sits on the couch and kicks off her shoes. The only thing she misses about India is her servants—her feet hurt from her heels and she wants a foot massage. This monologue is intended for an Indian performer.

God, I am so tired … just want to grab a bite and sleep …

She finds a packet of bhujia, rips it open, eats a mouthful.

This fried bhujia is totally addictive—you can't stop until you've finished the whole packet. I didn't eat this shit in India—we had a cook and a fleet of servants who cooked three meals a day.

She picks up a bottle of wine.

I don't trust my second-hand fridge—better finish the wine before it goes bad.

She drinks.

Just what I need after a long day. I hadn't tasted wine before I came here. Girls are not allowed to drink in our family—no drinks, no short skirts, and *no boyfriends*. Except me, all the girls in the family have had to settle for an arranged marriage. They had *no* takers—all the boys were after me. One of my cousins is getting married to an ugly billionaire. She's happy, it's the easiest way to become rich. The whole family's shopping for the wedding and posting their photos on Instagram, but my cousin's the limit.

She scrolls on her phone.

She posts her photos every ten minutes—Jeez! She's looking ugly in her red *lehenga*, and the number of likes she's got. People are so disingenuous on social media. My red *lehenga*'s so much better and my picture got 287 likes. I had worn it on my engagement. We had so much fun on my wedding—there was nonstop music, dance, party and *masti* for one whole week.

Ttt. [*With a sigh*] I really wanted to attend my cousin's wedding but uncle hasn't invited me. He says I am a bad influence on other girls. My mother requested my cousin to invite me unofficially, like she's inviting her friends, but she refused—Bitch! My mother's so upset—I hope she's not pleading with my grandfather again. I have to stop Ma before she makes me a laughing stock.

I call my mother and my brother takes the call—

Kamina. He thinks he can spit in my face because I made one mistake. Everybody makes mistakes, but my family is so unforgiving. My father is still angry I dropped out of college. I hated History, I slept through the lectures, I didn't want to waste my time doing something I didn't like, so I stopped going to college. I know it's good to have a degree, but it's my family—they oppose everything I do. They even opposed my marriage to Vivek. 'Vivek is not rich', said my father. But I liked Vivek, and more than Vivek I liked the idea of moving to Australia. And really, if they thought Vivek was a mistake they should have been happy when I divorced him, but they had a *huge* problem with my divorce. Tttt … I know I shouldn't have had an affair with Ricky whilst I was still married to Vivek but—okay, that was one mistake, but I corrected my mistake and moved in with Ricky. And now my family thinks Ricky was the *biggest* mistake of my life. At least I had the courage to end my marriage. I was clean—one man at a time, Ricky in, Vivek out. Besides, I was bored with Vivek. There were no beaches, no wine, no parties, no kangaroos, not even Australian friends. We stayed at home and …

Vivek was a misfit. He couldn't get into the rhythm of Melbourne. I belong here—Australia is the country of my *soul*. Some people can't dance to the beat of the city—but my family doesn't understand this. I don't care if I am not invited to family weddings, at least I am free to live and love. And *love, I will*.

She swigs wine from the bottle.

PETRA

From *Brothers Wreck*

by Jada Alberts

Brothers Wreck is a naturalistic play about Indigenous youth suicide and how families stick together. This scene is set in Adele's home in Darwin. Her aunty Petra, in her 40s, has just arrived after the long drive—she is there because Adele's mum is sick in hospital. In this scene she is speaking to Adele. This is a close family—they have been through hell and there is a lot of love holding them together. This monologue is intended for an Australian Indigenous performer.

You're probably too young to remember what happened on the Stuart—

Enough time's passed and you start to think, 'I've got a handle on this, I know what to do with this', but it's been fifteen years and still… Grief's a slippery little sucker with a mind of its own.

There's no way to avoid it, that stretch of highway. Sometimes in life you get to hide from things you don't wanna see, but there's no hidin from that accident. Even when I fly over I know exactly when I'm passin that place, can feel it in my bones. Doesn't matter if I'm asleep or nothin, I'll wake up to feel that feeling.

Beat.

So I called your mother this time, 'Isabel, I'm driving this time, no more planes! I'm driving'.

Beat.

I took the most beautiful flowers I could find in all of Alice Springs, natives of course, 'cause they last longer, and I laid them to rest right there at your aunty's cross beside that solid tree.

Was a funeral we was drivin from… Funeral, funeral, who was it now?

Beat.

Ah, my uncle, your nanna's eldest brother, my second pop, beautiful man your Uncle Errol.

God, all these funerals, ay, stand like signposts, don't they?… Along the way.

Beat.

We was travellin in convoy, us three sisters, coming back from funeral in Alice.

Your Aunty Lou wanted to get back quick 'cause your brother had been accepted to start school early. She thought Ruben was the smartest kid on the block. Had such high hopes, bless her… See, your brother was always tellin us these weird things. He loved science, planets and that. 'The universe, Aunty, is the biggest thing ever! Even bigger than Darwin!' Lou swore black and blue that kid would be the first blackfella in space. Hah! True God.

Beat.

Skies shoulda been clear but that year the wet broke so early we coulda swam home. Three cars, your Aunty Lou in front with Ruben. We'd stopped in Daly Waters for a feed, musta been about nine, piled all you kids back in the car, thought we'd push on another few hundred clicks—everyone seemed clear. Good.

Just before midnight it happened. Thought we'd cleared the rain but a storm front hit us hard south of Katherine. Road took us right into the belly of it. And what a belly it was.

Beat.

Me and Alley were number two in the convoy, and we seen something strange up ahead, a blurry little blemish between the blades of the busted wipers. And there he was, this drenched little boy, tossed about in the storm.

Beat.

I dream of him out there still, the world closing in on him. He was so terrifyingly small. High beams hit him and I thought I was dreamin. Alley lays on the brakes and sure enough, it's him, out there, in the middle of the black road.

Beat.

Your brother looked like a ghost, Del, if it wasn't for the blood, I would've sworn he was a ghost.

Beat.

We stopped. I grabbed him. Stripped him down to his gundies to check him, didn't have more than a scratch. Put him in the back seat. Your Uncle Alley followed the tracks goin off the road and Louise, my dear Lou. She wasn't wearing her belt.

Beat.

In my dreams it's the most peaceful thing.

Pause.

I hope she didn't wake up from that sleep. I hope that tree came and took her while she flew. That's how I like to think of it, anyway. Took her up, took her back, took her to that next place.

Beat.

Doesn't take much, does it. For the universe to tip on its head?

WOMAN

From *Money*

by Patricia Cornelius

In *Who's Afraid of the Working Class?*

by Andrew Bovell, Patricia Cornelius, Melissa Reeves and Christos Tsiolkas

Who's Afraid of the Working Class? *is a series of short plays, all dealing with characters in a state of social, economic and moral deprivation. This is the closing scene of the play. We know from the previous scenes that the woman is married and has a son, Daniel, referred to below. She and her husband have no other work and struggle to pay the mortgage. In an earlier scene with her husband and son she is abrasive, suspicious and desperate. The sick man has bought her tenderness. The scene is set in a bedroom. 'The woman sits up suddenly in the bed. She has just awoken. She quickly checks the time on her watch and then she relaxes. There is a sleeping man lying next to her. She gently leans over him and listens to his breathing.'*

Sleep. Sleep.

She touches his face. She gets up, careful not to disturb the sleeping man.

He fell at my feet. Never had a man fall at my feet before. He literally fell, at my feet, in the street. In Sydney Road. Of all the people he could have fallen in front of, he chose me. And I thought: Fuck! Why me?! I tried to get other people to help but not on your life, they weren't going to have a bar of him or me. Probably thought he was drunk. I did. I said, get up, you silly bugger, get up. But he was sick, not drunk, sick and he asked me to call him a taxi and by the time one of them took notice of me and pulled over, he was up on his feet but real groggy and looking drunker than drunk and the taxi driver was shaking his head and the only way I could get him to take him was if I got in too. So I took him home and he only lives two streets away from me so it wasn't any big deal. I helped him inside and on to this bed. And then I said, I've got to go. Will you be all right? I've got to go. I wanted to get out of there before he got more sick or he died or something. Then he opened his eyes, his beautiful eyes and he thanked me. He got out his wallet and I said, don't be silly. I don't want your money. You gave me a lift. I only live two streets away. But he insisted and he took out two hundred dollars and held it out to me. I couldn't believe my eyes. Two hundred dollars! You've got to be kidding. Is this bloke an easy take or what? I said, no, I couldn't. Two hundred dollars, on a silver platter being offered to me. It was like a miracle. That's all I needed. Two hundred dollars. I was short two hundred dollars. With that two hundred dollars I could pay that month's mortgage. It was kind of like it was meant to be. No, I couldn't, I said. And I took it. And I paid the mortgage. But I didn't feel good. I could barely eat or sleep. What's it matter, I thought. He offered it to me. I did him a good turn. I came back to tell him that I was so sorry I took his money. His door was open and I found him here where I'd last seen him. Asleep. And I thought what's sorry going to do, so I cleaned his house and I washed his clothes and I cooked him something to eat. When he woke he smiled when he saw me and went back to sleep. I came back the next day and the day after that. I've been coming for almost a year. No one knows I come. Only him and me know. When the district nurse comes I hide out the back until she's gone. One day she came early and I was in bed and I pulled the sheet over my head and lay as still as death and listened to her prattle on about it being time for him to give it up and come into hospital. He got the giggles and she asked him what he found so funny and checked to see if he was getting too much morph. On good days we sit and talk. He asks me about me. What about me, I say. Anything, he says. And so I tell him anything, anything that comes into my mind. Sometimes I fall asleep too. He's in my arms and it's so lovely and warm, I feel myself go. It's irresistible. I think I sleep more sound here than in my own bed at home. Some days there's no talk and no sleep. Painful days. Now he's smaller I cup him into me and I whisper, sh, sh, sh, shush now, shush now, and I think I'm holding my baby. My sweet little boy. My Daniel. How long since I held you? And then I think, who's got the pain here, me or you? Sometimes when I hold him and at last he gets some relief and sleeps, I lie there and I imagine I'm having an affair. And we've just made passionate love. If I could I would make love to him. If his body wasn't quite so tired. When his body touches mine, the warmth of him, and his breathing, gentle as it is, is enough. I come. I do. You smell nice, he says to me, when he wakes sometimes. And I laugh. He pays me. I should be paying you, I think when I pocket it. He pays me for the cleaning, the cooking, for the company. I can't tell anyone that I come here. I can't. What could I say? I've got a job. What do you do, they'd ask. I couldn't explain it. I don't like to call it a job, it doesn't feel like a job. I like to get the money but I think he'd give it to me anyway.

She lifts the blankets and crawls into the bed next to him.

CHRISTIE

From *Mother*

by Daniel Keene

Mother *is a one-woman play that tells the story of Christie. She is about sixty and homeless. In the character description it says: 'Her hair is long and unkempt. She wears a ragged, floral patterned dress that reaches to the ground. Her feet are bare, almost black with dirt.' As she recounts the following, she is 'Inside a derelict house. Cold rooms. Rats scratching. Stains.' Lenny and the baby were living at his sister's house, with Christie allowed to visit the baby once a week. Mrs Kennedy was the neighbour who gave Christie alcohol when she 'needs a bit of relief'.*

When Lenny stopped paying the rent on the house I went round to his sister's place to see him and he wouldn't even let me inside
so I stood there on the front step like a fucking beggar
and he told me that I could move in with him and his sister
there was a sleepout I could have
he wasn't paying for a place where he didn't live
and I said aren't you coming back
but he didn't answer
you'd be close to the baby was all he said
and so you and your sister can keep eye on me I said
I'm thinking about you and the baby he said
oh yeah I said

I might as well be a corpse as in that sleepout I said
what kind of life would I have living like that out the back
with eyes on me day and night
what kind of a life have you got now he said
my own life I said
I want what's best he said
best for who I said not for me I said
for the baby for the baby he said
pig's arse I said
he should be with me I said
he should be with his mother
Christie he said
Christie have you looked at yourself lately
every morning when I have a wash I said
I see myself staring back
I see that baby's mother
I see empty arms where a baby should be
I see hands with nothing to do
I see a mouth that hasn't been kissed
I'm dried out with crying I said
I'm heavy inside like someone's cut me open and stitched a lead weight inside me
like someone's taken a stick to me
look in my eyes Lenny
look in my eyes and tell me what you see
/
he didn't say nothing for a while
he wouldn't look at me
you can move into the sleepout any time you want he said
what if I don't want to I said
then I don't know what you'll do he said

and that was the end of it
he turned away shut the door
/
I went home and looked at myself
I wanted to see what Lenny had seen
something had made him turn away from me
but how can you turn away from yourself
you've got to see yourself when you're not looking
you've got to look at yourself as though you're someone else
how can you do that
/
I sat on the back step of the house that wasn't mine anymore
I sat there as night-time filled the backyard
all the green weeds and the flowers I'd planted
and the vegetables dying in the plots that Lenny had dug
were all disappearing into the dark
and I tried to see myself
to see what Lenny saw and what my mother saw
and what the baby saw
I saw my hands on Lenny's skin
and my hands holding the baby's tiny hands
and I saw my arms around my mother
helping her into bed and all her ruined life like sweat on her skin
and I saw my face against Lenny's face
on our pillows in our bed in our house that wasn't ours anymore
and I saw my baby's face still raw from being inside me pressed into my soft belly
and I saw my arms red from the hot water in the trough
and my hands wringing out the sheets and hanging them on the clothesline
I saw my face rounded on the side of an empty bottle
and staring at me from the window of the Rising Sun Hotel

I saw my face bruised by the back of my father's hand
and I saw my face kissed by Lenny
I saw my face in the black glass of the kitchen window when the night was late
and I was sat there my hands on my knees and my hair hanging down
and the baby crying in the front room
I saw my face the way I'd never seen it and the way I'd always seen it
and I looked out into the backyard
where the washing on the clothesline flapped like a bird against the cold of the sky
and that was all I saw
/
I don't remember the next days
just Mrs Kennedy feeding me the good stuff
me not much of myself just in pieces
and the looks of neighbours
like sharpened knives when I shut the house behind me
and left for good
/
I left the key in the door
I never went back
nobody lived there anymore

ANTIGONE

From *Antigone*
by Damien Ryan

Damien Ryan's adaptation of Sophocles' classic play is set in a modern war zone and explores higher principles than can sometimes be reflected in written law. Antigone is sentenced to death for attempting to bury her brother, a 'terrorist', and in so doing breaking the law of her uncle. In this scene, Antigone has been sentenced to death. She is making love to Haemon and has, in a sense, left her body to address the audience. As she speaks, she is making a noose. Ismene is her sister.

Who are you?

Are you the future—are they talking to the future, trying to teach you something? Or is it like history? Are you just recording it, all the sordid details—the inbred girl who ruined everyone's day—just recording it, for a library somewhere.

I know you're there.

And while my boy there, my love, makes a woman out of me, I'm gonna say a few things.

She watches him / them.

I wish I could enjoy it more but I have a lot on my mind—

She sits down.

So—this is my lament. My name is Antigone. [*A great vulnerability in her*]

I wish I could surprise you and not die. But I know my destiny. Even my name means, 'worthy of one's parents' …! It's in my blood. I nearly gave blood yesterday. [*Showing us the black letters on her arm*] I chickened out, I thought if they tested my blood, they'd find I was prehistoric.

That's why I lied to Ismene when she asked where our father was. I saw my destiny, as we walked. He was spared the sight, lucky prick. Plague and death everywhere, bloated death. I told Ismene he died happy, that he'd found joy; he didn't, he just screamed and screamed, like a child, the pain in his eyes. In the end I couldn't stand it, I just stopped walking, let go of his hand, and kept moving as he grabbed for me—like two kids playing blind man's bluff in the desert. He screamed some more—screamed my name—'worthy of one's parents', 'Worthy of one's parents!', that's all *I* heard—he cried for me and cursed me, but I just sat down and stared at a rock, just watched the sun move. People think I was loyal. But he was just a selfish old man.

[*Quickly now*] Not that my story is special. So many children have died here—there's nothing special about me. I hope the others get to talk to you too—but I just want to say this …

There are three things I'll miss out on that I wish I could have. I'll never be married. I'll never make a child, my own little thing, to hold.

Looking back at Haemon who is moving under the blanket:

Maybe there's a seed now, maybe my body is starting a process as we speak—as I speak.

Shielding her eyes from the light to look for the audience:

I hope someone's out there. Maybe it's happening already while he's inside me. Like how stars form—I loved this at school—molecular clouds—that's all pushing and pulling too. Gravity pulls in harder than the pressure is able to push out and the cloud collapses. Everything heats up and just gives way, there's no explosion, no great climax, that's a bit of a myth I think, things just … happen at a steady pace … and as it all dies down the hot core at the heart of the cloud sticks together, a little protostar—a thing that will *one day* be a star. Nothing much to look at, but one day … like the dragonflies. The rest of the cloud doesn't go to waste either, all that dust makes comets and whole planets, whole worlds just from the *debris*, everything counts up there, every little thing—a promise, a dead brother—nothing goes to waste up there. Down here though …

That's why I buried my brother, because, beyond the possibilities of my intuition, I knew what I did was right.

Oh, he's finishing. I have to go. I want to say goodbye.

The third thing I'll miss? I just wanted to see what life was like—I kept waiting for a time when I'd see it, for myself—just to live.

Goodbye.

MOT

From *Highway of Lost Hearts*
by Mary Anne Butler

Highway of Lost Hearts *is a one-woman show that follows Mot on her journey through Australia, in search of her own, and her country's, heart. It takes her from Darwin to Sydney. There is a lot about Mot (and Australia) that can be deduced from the following passage, which opens the play. It is quickly established that Mot is intuitive and introspective, earthy and humorous, and, above all, brave.*

I wake up one morning to find that my heart is missing
from my chest.
I can breathe, I have a pulse, but I feel…
nothing.
So. I decide to go and look for it. I pack up my van, hoick the dog up into the passenger seat, and head down the Highway of Lost Hearts.
And as I reach the outskirts of this city, I realise that my heart has been missing for some time.
Or if not missing, then at least…
empty.

At Katherine, I stop for provisions. I leave the dog in the car with a bowl of water and the windows open, and promise her a bone from the fresh meat section on my return.

As I juggle my goods back to the car, a can of tomatoes falls at the feet of a woman in a wheelchair. I bend to pick up the can and offer her a small smile of apology.

She reaches out a gnarled claw at me; upturned and fused like a dead inverted crab.

And I think: she wants money.

But no.

She's trying to touch me.

And my body jerks itself backwards and I'm up on my feet, walking away.

… leaving my tomatoes lying there.

The dog greets me with a thump of her tail, and asks me where the bone is.

I tell her she's not eating it in the front seat. She can have it when we stop.

… and she sulks all the way into the next town…

At Mataranka we dwell amongst a motley collection of gravestones, glowing in the heat of the day. The dog hunkers down with her bone while I wander through the plots, bringing the names of dead people back to life:

Burkey the Builder

Ginty

Bruno Kutschki

Doogs—all 21 years of him

KW—no date, no name

Elisa Lambert; born seventh of the third, 1982; deceased eleventh of the third, 1982

—and the shock of her five short days on this earth makes me look away.

The slideshow starts inside my head:

Night.

Ocean.

A body: floating.

Ruptured; wafting and shapeless.

There is no map for this journey.

The dog huffs at me; her jaws bloodied. I haul her twenty-seven kilos up into the jump seat, and she issues happy meaty farts all the way to Larrimah.

At the Daly Waters pub, a curtain of bras hangs down from the ceiling. A bearded, barefoot version of Wild Bill Hickok straddles a bar stool; a stubby of Fourex fused to his hand. 'I Eat Pussy' proud across his chest. I ask him if he's seen any hearts pass by this way, and he leans towards me like he's got a secret:

'Dunno about hearts, love. But you'd be wantin' to find some mojo first, wouldn'tcha?'

He pisses himself laughing and goes back to his beer, tipping it upright and draining the last dregs before calling for another.

I go back to my van and add 'find mojo' to my list.

And as I drive, I think of dead people.

The weight of them in the silence of my dreams.

A ute full of young blokes passes, pig dogs in cages on the back. Rifles primed, 'Khe Sanh' blaring out. One of them checks me out as they pass, but I'm invisible: too old for desire, and too young for ridicule—so he averts his head, cracks a stubby and drinks instead to the passing tarmac. White lines like a road map, towards his next kill.

The dog picks up the scent of the pig dogs and props up, ears alert, whimpering to go on the hunt as well.

No.

Sit.

SIT!

I teach her to drink from a plastic water bottle while we drive. It rests at her paws and she licks it when she wants a drink. I pop open the nozzle and squeeze it while she schlurps the drops. If I do it too fast, it goes up her nose and she issues a snuffle-cough, so I slow down. Gradually, we get the pace right and work together in a soft rhythm until she turns her head to one side, refusing to schlurp any more.

As night draws close along the Highway of Lost Hearts I stop in at Dunmarra to camp for the night.

I wait at the counter while this big bloke ambles across…

'Drivin'?' he says.

'No,' I say. 'Teleporting.'

'Smartarse as well?'

'Ah… fair enough. Fuel, thanks. And a stubby of Coopers Green.'

'You out here all alone, are ya?'

'No. I've got a dog. A big dog.'

He nods, holds out my change but won't let it go.

'Where ya stayin'?'

'Um… not sure.'

'Well, the next town's Elliot. It's a blackfella town, just so's ya know.'

'Well, they were there first. So yeah; I guess it is.'

He goes suddenly still. 'You wanna watch it,' he whispers. 'A girlie could get herself in trouble talking like that, way out here.'

He puts my change down on the counter halfway between us, so that I have to reach towards him if I want it.

'Right,' I say. 'Okay. Thanks for the warning.'

… and I leave my change lying there…

Down the track me and the dog pull over to rough-camp it for the night. I hide the van behind some scrub, lock the doors, wind the windows up and keep the dog close by.

Late in the night she lets out a long, low growl.

… and all night long, I feel like I'm being watched…

SAPPHO

From *Sappho ... in 9 Fragments* by Jane Montgomery Griffiths

This is the poet Sappho, tenth muse of the ancient Greeks, speaking today after 2700 years of interpretation and reinterpretation. The papier mâché that she refers to is the papyrus rolls that her poetry was originally written on. In Griffiths' interpretation, Sappho is not particularly pleasant, but she is (to quote from Griffiths' own introduction) 'highly intelligent, highly charismatic, witty, urbane, detached, desperate, needy, resentful, angry, immature, sophisticated, bemused, judgemental, conservative, snobbish, yearning, bereft'.

The rainy Pleiads wester
And seek beyond the sea
The head that I shall dream on
That 'twill not dream of me.

I hope that was not rain. Not good for me to get too soggy… papier mâché.

'If we read Sappho without prejudice, we observe that she is deeply moved by the physical graces of young women.' Denys Page, another of my ventriloquist lovers, Cambridge Don, scholar, Fellow, author of learned commentaries on Ionian lyric poets—not one to suffer fools gladly, but always such a gentleman to me… rubbing ankles in the Copper Kettle over eccles cakes and frothy coffee… always paid and held the door—wanted so badly to make an honest woman of me… 'It is a lover's passion, not sisterly affection or maternal benevolence, which Sappho describes in Fragment 31, the overwhelming emotion of intensest love.'

Having said that, there is no evidence to justify the accusation that she was 'addicted to the perversion which the modern world names after her native island'.

With friends like that, who needs enemies?

Once upon a time, Sappho was the name of choice for girls born on the isle of Lesbos. Every family had a daughter named Sappho. But now—not now… now we have Electras, Antigones, Clytemnestras, Iphigenias… but never a Sappho. Better to name your daughter after a matricide than a lesbian. So I lose one habitat and find another: exiled from my homeland, I find sanctuary with the daughters of Lesbos. My homeland becomes synonymous for 'women who love women'. Orientation replaces location. Caps lock to lower case. 'Lesbian' is no longer a nationality; it is an irrationality. An affliction, a perversion, an aberration against God. A turn-off… a turn-on. A condemnation… a celebration. To the wider world, I am a dangerous model, but to the daughters of Lesbos, I am their mother. Welcome home, Mummy! I become a lesbian icon: Martina Navratilova, k d lang, Jodie Foster, Peppermint Patty… and me…

By now, of course, I have no body. No material volume, just voluminous emptiness. Shards and fragments passed down by others. Enough to wet the lips but leave the palate dry. Fragment (consider revising). Fragment (consider discarding). Fragment (consider rewriting). Oh how tantalising. The scent of gossip. Just a scent, but that's all they need. The slightest waft of scandal and saucy little rumours to give spice to my spaces.

So that's what they did. Words fail, but rumours survive. Not coming from me. Not from my words. Not from my passions. From theirs. All theirs.

Notorious for sexual decadence, I am fair game, they think. Notorious for sexual depravity, I will like being used, they think. Again and again they enter my emptiness; fill my dark nothingness with their own pressing need; plant sordid seeds of longing in my fecund silent cave. They fuck me with desire and I become all things to all men… and women.

Etre Sappho ce serait être tout le monde—Being Sappho might just be the future of the world…

1759. Naples. Pompeii. Look at me now… now you see me, now you don't. I am unearthed, uncovered… here I am, staring out at you. Bet you didn't recognise me. Here I am with my stylus, with my dark hair (and I'm not a bit ugly, and you can't tell that I am short). Here I am, sucking my pencil like any diligent schoolgirl, looking for the answer to life's thorny tests… *il ritratto di Saffo – Portrait of Sappho –* first century AD, Roman fresco, enlightenment pin-up and Sapphic red herring… Of course, it's seven hundred years out of date, and two seas and two mainlands out of location (dislocated—all those limbs torn again), it's the wrong language and the girl is writing, it's the wrong country and the girl is younger… but no matter… the smiling girl was Sappho—my face was reborn.

Quite the thing, you know, to be painted as me/as her—they all did it, all those aristocratic, transvestite ladies, crossing not gender but centuries. Attitudinising. Playing Sappho playing. Such lovely fantasies—these artists' wives who look to the distance, dreaming of the painter, the artist lover hopes (but I know differently)—a tamed Sappho, a polite Sappho. My limbs are put back together in these artists' models—lovely ladies of the enlightenment. I spread my limbs on cushions of down for the artist to make use of my body. And the artist, how he sighs; how he wears his longing on the sleeve in the delicate folds of muslin on skin.

These ladies will never escape the canvas, will never turn their heads to look out at you and ask you the reason for this passion. Look, they are trapped, and my limbs form the bars of their painted prison. Enlightenment butterflies pinned to the board. My passion, my longing, my breasts, my eyes—by your gaze, stolen. Tantalising and titillating. What erect bosoms, what stand-to-attention nipples. My tangential tits talk… much more than my words… because you have made me, trapped me, stopped my mouth… scroll, lyre, laurel leaf, volcano and silence.

But now here come the big boys: my Victorian masters. Virgin or whore; model or caution. Oh, those Victorians knew how to play with a story. So now I am split again. A virtuous poetess communing with my Muse; a sex-crazed whore brought low by lust. There I am now, there, do you see? I bend over so intently to listen to Alcaeus. Cleis stands by my side; my girls watch from behind. Look at the seats and you'll see the graffiti: a hundred loves carved into stone. But sacred love; Platonic love… with only… the faintest… hint… of… possibility… Oh, such torrid potential.

Voluptuous virgin or voracious vampire, take your pick, take your prick. There I am, there, there, do you see? The perverted, mad invert. Down on your knees… you witch bitch you dyke you deserve to be punished… prone and prostrate by the power of the penis. And there I am, there, there, do you see? Pray for forgiveness, you sad, shameful sinner… Think you'd preserve your depraved independence… Yes, that's right. Punish me, torture me, execute me, I deserve it—make me in thrall to a man who smells of bilge water; throw me from the cliff, for love of a redneck. Make me a psychotic, a mad woman, a suicide. An hysteric, you see how I arch my back? A depressive, you see how I drop my lyre? Come on, you can do more, you can do worse, out with your fantasies, punish me, punish me, BRING IT ON!

Her love, her leap, her looks and her lyrics… in that order. That is what I was to them.

The French were as bad, but a little more… open. They loved me… loved me. Revolutionary ladies in women-only salons: a model, a role model, a symbol of learning, a man-free utopia. But that didn't last for long. Napoleon and those that followed saw to that—clever women with independent tastes far too unsettling for the narcissistic gnome. So, a new story, now. Lost or lascivious. Flying to my watery death, or to my nubile lovers. Acrobatic aesthete or doomed, depraved decadent. Look, here comes Baudelaire! How he wishes he were lesbian! And look, there's Swinburne! (there, with the hair—he's not really French, I'm using poetic licence): how he wishes he were Baudelaire! Oh, how these naughty boys use me! 'Intolerable interludes, and infinite ill, amorous agonies with pangs too soft to kill.' Their Sadeian sidekick, sub/dom all in one, bruised lips, stinging veins to compound their fun… Mother of Latin games and lewd Greek love… Oh, I am suddenly immensely promiscuous—up for sale, spreading myself wide. Little figurines of me, made and sold all over Europe. Everyone wants a piece of me. Even the Germans.

I am found and lost a thousand times.

And none of them really knows me.

ROSIE

From *Things I Know To Be True*
by Andrew Bovell

We've broken our own rule to include this second monologue from Things I Know To Be True, *but I'm sure you'll understand why when you read the monologue below. Rosie, Pip's sister, is 19 and on her first trip overseas.*

Berlin. A winter coat. A travel bag. A red nose. And a broken heart.

I'm standing on the platform at the train station. It's cold. The train is late and my socks are wet. I'm not quite sure how I got here or where I'm meant to go next.

I met him four nights ago and he was the most beautiful boy I had ever seen. His name was Emmanuel, of course, and he came from Madrid.

I'd been travelling by myself for three months. The great European adventure. London. Dublin. Paris. Prague. Then Berlin. I'd been saving for a year. Cafe work, bar work, babysitting. Mum and Dad said don't go by yourself. It's too dangerous. Go on a tour or at least with some girlfriends.

I'll meet people. I told them. I'll be fine. But meeting people is harder than you think. I mean I did, meet people, at hostels and stuff but mainly other Australians. And it was fun for a night or two. But the boys just wanted to have sex and I guess that's alright but if I wanted sex with an Australian boy I would have stayed in Hallett Cove.

So I go to the churches and the museums and the galleries and I walk through the cobbled streets and I sit in cafes trying to look mysterious and everything is so beautiful. Everything is what I was expecting it to be. And yet somehow I want it to be more.

I Skype home twice a week and tell Mum and Dad what an amazing place Europe is. They've never been. I tell them I'm having the best time because I can't bear the thought of them being disappointed for me. And when I Skype my brother Mark, I pretend the camera on my iPad is broken because he knows me and he will see it in my face. He'll see that it's all a mess and he'll tell me to come home but I can't go home, not yet, I mean then, I couldn't go home then because it would be such a … defeat.

I don't know what it's meant to be. I don't know what I'm meant to do. I keep wondering when it will start. Life. When will life start?

And then there he is. At a club in Mitte. Dancing. With his shirt off. And I think, wow, that guy can really dance. That guy is like … fire. And then he looks over at me. Me? And I am gone. I pretend not to be. I try to be cool. To make it seem like I'm not interested. But I am so interested. And we dance until the sun comes up. And as we come out of the club into the light, I think this is it. This is life. I am living.

And I know he wants to take me home. To his place. Or to his friend's place. Or to someone's place, I'm not quite sure whose place it is, and I say okay. Because at last I am living and I don't want life to stop.

And when he kisses me I want to cry. Because I'd never been kissed like that. Not in Hallett Cove. And I'd never been kissed where he kissed me or touched quite like that. He seemed to know things and for once it didn't seem to matter that I didn't. Three days. Three days we stayed in bed. And after three days I knew some things too.

We don't even get up to eat. He disappears and comes back with a bowl of cereal and two spoons. And that's all we eat. Cereal. Out of the same bowl. For three days.

On the third night I watch him sleeping and I do that thing you shouldn't do. I think about the future. I imagine taking him home to meet Mum and Dad and my sister and brothers and and and how they will all love him, like they love me. And how clever I am and brave to have found such a man, such a beautiful man, different but the same, and brought him all the way back to Hallett Cove and then, there I am … Oh, I am so embarrassed but suddenly there I am in our backyard with Dad's roses all around us and I'm walking across the lawn on his arm, and he's got tears in his eyes and Mum's there in a new dress, which she never lets herself have, and my sister Pip is there with her husband, Steve, and their two girls. She got married in the backyard too. And Mark, my oldest brother who I adore is there with his girlfriend, Taylor. And then there's Ben, my other brother who's there with a girl who's new and won't last because they just don't with Ben and I love them all so much, sometimes I think, too much, if you can love too much, but now I have to make room for Emmanuel who's standing there in a suit and he is just so, so … so handsome … And I … I'm wearing a white dress … And I'm kind of surprised, kind of shocked because I never even knew that that's what I wanted. And maybe it's not what I want, it's what I think Mum and Dad will want for me, but anyway I'm there in a white dress on my father's arm walking across the lawn and …

Then he wakes up and he looks at me as if he knows what I'm thinking and as if he wants to get up and run, so I kiss him on his lips before he can. And he smiles. And I'm gone all over again. And we make love, so tenderly, so sweetly, and after, as I drift off to sleep, lying on his chest, listening to the beat of his heart, thinking I could listen to this for the rest of my life, I think is this it, is this what falling in love is?

And when I wake up in the morning he's gone … along with four hundred Euros from my wallet, my iPad, my camera, my favourite scarf and a large piece of my heart. I find a girl in the house, smoking a cigarette at the kitchen table, and ask if she's seen him. She shrugs and says that he said something about going to see his girlfriend in London. She tells me to get my things and to get out of her house.

I walk through the streets of Berlin. I feel small. I feel like I'm twelve years old, I feel ridiculous. I want to cry but I won't. Well I do, a bit. But not as much as I want to. I want my dad. I want my mum. I want my brothers and my sister. I want to hear them laugh and argue and fight and tease me. But I can't think of them much because if I do my chest will explode. I feel like I'm going to literally fall to pieces. That my arms are going to drop off and then my legs and my head. And so to stop myself coming apart I make a list of all the things I know … I mean actually know for certain to be true, and the really frightening thing is … it's a very short list.

I don't know much at all.

But I know that at twenty-five Windarie Avenue, Hallett Cove, things are the same as when I left and they always will be.

And I know that I have to go home.

SOURCES

Abela, D. (2017). *Jump for Jordan* (revised edition). Currency Press, pp. 20–21. Copyright © Donna Abela. Extract reprinted by permission of the author.

Alberts, J. (2015). *Brothers Wreck*. Currency Press, pp. 22–24. Copyright © Jada Alberts. Extract reprinted by permission of the author.

Betzien, A. (2017). *The Hanging*. Currency Press, pp. 36–37. Copyright © Angela Betzien. Extract reprinted by permission of the author.

Bovell, A. (2017). *Things I Know To Be True*. Currency Press, pp. 3–5 and 17–18. Copyright © Andrew Bovell. Extract reprinted by permission of the author.

Bubnic, M. (2013). *Beached*. Currency Press, pp. 22–24. Copyright © Melissa Bubnic. Extract reprinted by permission of the author.

Butler, M. A. (2014). *Highway of Lost Hearts*. Currency Press, pp. 1–4. Copyright © Mary Anne Butler. Extract reprinted by permission of the author.

Campbell, J. & Hamilton, S. (2017). *They Saw a Thylacine*. Published in Campbell, C., Hamilton, S., Lewis, C. & Rayson, H., *Endangered*. Currency Press, pp. 41–45. Copyright © Justine Campbell and Sarah Hamilton. Extract reprinted by permission of the authors.

Carleton, S. (2016). *The Turquoise Elephant*. Currency Press, pp. 40–41. Copyright © Stephen Carleton. Extract reprinted by permission of the author.

Chaplin, A., Mazzella, K. & Thomson, K. (2003). *Mavis Goes To Timor*. Currency Press, pp. 8–9. Copyright © Angela Chaplin, Kavisha Mazzella & Katherine Thomson. Extract reprinted by permission of the authors.

Coleman, E. (2003). *Secret Bridesmaids' Business*. Currency Press, p. 21. Copyright © Elizabeth Coleman. Extract reprinted by permission of the author.

Cornelius, P. (2000). *Money*. Published in Bovell, A., Cornelius, P., Reeves, M., Tsiolkas, C. & Vela, I., *Who's Afraid of the Working Class?*. Currency Press, pp. 65–67. Copyright © Patricia Cornelius. Extract reprinted by permission of the author.

Cornelius, P. (2017). *SHIT*. Published in Badham, V., Barnes, A. & Cornelius, P., *Muff / MinusOneSister / SHIT*. Currency Press, pp. 127–128. Copyright © Patricia Cornelius. Extract reprinted by permission of the author.

Enoch, W. (2007). *Black Medea*. Currency Press, pp. 77–79. Copyright © Wesley Enoch. Extract reprinted by permission of the author.

Griffiths, J. M. (2010). *Sappho … in 9 Fragments*. Currency Press, pp. 23–26. Copyright © Jane Montgomery Griffiths. Extract reprinted by permission of the author.

Kalsie, R. N. (2017). *Melbourne Talam*. Currency Press, pp. 5–8. Copyright © Rashma N. Kalsie. Extract reprinted by permission of the author.

Keene, D. (2015). *Mother*. Currency Press, pp. 29–32. Copyright © Daniel Keene. Extract reprinted by permission of the author.

Kruckemeyer, F. (2013). *At Sea, Staring Up*. Currency Press, pp. 5–7. Copyright © Finegan Kruckemeyer. Extract reprinted by permission of the author.

Miller, S. (2017). *Sunset Strip*. Currency Press, pp. 50–52. Copyright © Suzie Miller. Extract reprinted by permission of the author.

Mulvany, K. & Silvey, C. (2017). *Jasper Jones* (revised edition). Currency Press, pp. 66–67. Copyright © Kate Mulvany & Craig Silvey. Extract reprinted by permission of the authors.

O'Connell, T. (2004). *Minefields and Miniskirts*. Currency Press, pp. 4–8. Copyright © Terence O'Connell. Extract reprinted by permission of the author.

Oswald, D. (2007). *The Peach Season*. Currency Press, pp. 15–16, 71–72. Copyright © Debra Oswald. Extract reprinted by permission of the author.

Philpott, L. (2014). *Truck Stop*. Currency Press, pp. 1–3. Copyright © Lachlan Philpott. Extract reprinted by permission of the author.

Purcell, L. (2017). *The Drover's Wife* (revised edition). Currency Press, pp. 16–17. Copyright © Leah Purcell. Extract reprinted by permission of the author.

Reid, C. (2010). *Prayer to an Iron God*. Currency Press, p. 1. Copyright © Caroline Reid. Extract reprinted by permission of the author.

Ryan, D. (2017). *Antigone*. Published in Ryan, D., *Antigone / Cyrano de Bergerac*. Currency Press, pp. 57–59. Copyright © Damien Ryan. Extract reprinted by permission of the author.

Sabawi, S. (2016). *Tales of a City by the Sea*. Currency Press, pp. 28–29. Copyright © Samah Sabawi. Extract reprinted by permission of the author.

Sewell, S. (2003). *Myth, Propaganda and Disaster in Nazi Germany and Contemporary America*. Currency Press, pp. 38–39. Copyright © Stephen Sewell. Extract reprinted by permission of the author.

Tersman, N. (2017). *Parasites*. Currency Press, pp. 28–31. Copyright © Ninna Tersman. Extract reprinted by permission of the author.

Valentine, A. (2017). *Letters to Lindy*. Currency Press, pp. 11–12. Copyright © Alana Valentine. Extract reprinted by permission of the author.

RELATED TITLES FROM CURRENCY PRESS

Not in the Script

John McCallum & Jenny Nicholls

This monologue collection offers up a challenge: to perform with voices that aren't from play scripts. Working instead from fiction, non-fiction and poetry, these pieces are a fresh and sharp source of material for performance, auditions and workshops. Unusual sources provide the actor or drama student with a new array of monologue possibilities.

The characters range from lovers in the *King James Bible* to a sci-fi Artificial Intelligence unit navigating gender identities between planets. Classic sources include *Great Expectations, Jane Eyre, Ulysses* and *The Bell Jar* and work from Beckett, Kafka and Mark Twain. Strong contemporary monologues come from work by Raymond Carver, Miranda July, Elena Ferrante, Jeffrey Eugenides, Alice Munro and David Sedaris. Australian voices speak in iconic moments from *Jasper Jones* and John Marsden's Tomorrow series and from definitive work by David Malouf, Elizabeth Jolley, Geraldine Brooks, Morris Gleitzman, Jeanine Leane, Gayle Kennedy and Alice Pung.

These monologues speak from moments of radical change and subtle exploration. Beneath each is a well-crafted literary work with its own world of characters, conflicts and tension: we invite you to look beyond the script.

978-1-92500-583-7, also available as a digital edition.

The Actor's Audition Manual

Dean Carey

The first edition of *The Actor's Audition Manual* quickly became known as the 'red audition bible', making it the essential guide. Now revised, it brings together a wealth of practical advice and a fresh range of speeches from Australian plays that will help make any audition powerful and effective. **NEW EDITION COMING MAY 2018 (print and digital).**

FOR MORE MONOLOGUES & FULL SCRIPTS FOR ALL PLAYS FEATURED IN THIS COLLECTION, SEE OUR WEBSITE:

WWW.CURRENCY.COM.AU